Hungry Ghosts

Hungry Ghosts

Poems by

Cindy Buchanan

Cover design by Shay Culligan
Cover image by Roman Melnychuk on Unsplash
Author photo by Scott Buchanan

ISBN: 979-8-90146-714-5
Library of Congress Control Number: 2026931899

Kelsay Books
502 South 1040 East, A-119
American Fork, Utah 84003
Kelsaybooks.com

For my husband, Scott

More Praise for Hungry Ghosts

Compelling, accessible, and remarkably honest, *Hungry Ghosts* is filled with stark, realistic, personal yet quite universal poems that paint an intimate portrait of identity, interpersonal struggles, loss, family, and the ever-present need for empathy. In these vibrant poems of community, nature, biography, Buchanan showcases a true talent for imbuing the smallest human details with authenticity and layered meanings. Each poem maps out the human heart in relation to that larger human heart we all share together, in all their internal conflicts, with precision and grace.

—John Sibley Williams, author, *As One Fire Consumes Another, The Drowning House*

Cindy Buchanan's *Hungry Ghosts* is a collection of poems that explore difficult subjects: childhood trauma, multi-generational searching and pain, to *be a mother who howls.* These poems take the reader on a candid journey of heartbreak and sorrow ultimately winding their way to a hard-found peace. And when solace does arrive it's often in nature. It's present in the moment where *There's a slight brown curling at the edge of the thornapple, and look, look, there's a spider spinning a web between flower and leaf.*

This is a poet who has done the hard work of writing through the weight of despair and hurt, and *for even the briefest moment,* has found *a more bearable lightness* that provides hope to all of us who struggle with our own grief.

—Carey Taylor, author, *The Lure of Impermanence, Some Aid to Navigation*

Acknowledgments

Many thanks to the editors of these journals in which versions of the following poems first appeared:

Bearing Witness: Poetry for Troubled Times (Sligo Creek Publishing): "A Wake," "A Necessary Ekphrasis"
Cirque: "Bonanza"
Evening Street Review: "Miss Olson at 59," "Perfume Bottle on the Windowsill"
The Fourth River: "January in the Park"
The Inflectionist Review: "Faith and Science," "Moonrise, Baja California Sur," "Paper Fortune Teller," "Old Enough" (printed as "Weight of Water")
Litmosphere!: "Here in the Land Where Desert Meets the Sea"
The MacGuffin: "Imagine My Surprise," "Hunger"
The Main Street Rag: "November Storm, Cloud Mountain Retreat," "Reclamation" (printed as "Stirring Memories")
One Art: "Named by All," "Summer Afternoon"
PentaCat Press: "Running in the Dark"
Plainsongs Poetry Journal: "Seal of Delight"
Rabid Oak: "In Praise of Glacial Movement," "The Lighthouse" (printed as "Chains of Love")
Tipton Poetry Journal: "Bardo," "First Rise," "What I Want"
Tupelo Quarterly: "Elemental"
Valparaiso Poetry Review: "Little Cabin in the Woods"

Some of these poems previously appeared in the author's chapbook, *Learning to Breathe* (Finishing Line Press, 2023).

I am indebted to my mother for my lifelong love of reading and music. My husband, Scott, has generously provided me with the time and space I need to write; I am grateful for his understanding and support. I am thankful to my dear friend, Anne Boyer, for her encouragement, and for her willingness to read and comment on poems in progress. I also appreciate the guidance of John Sibley Williams on early drafts of this manuscript. His suggestions gave me direction and focus.

Jeanine Walker has been and continues to be my amazing mentor. Her passion for poetry is contagious and her expectation for excellence has challenged me to become a better writer. Her classes provide a space where I can workshop poems and receive invaluable feedback on manuscript compilation. Many thanks to Jeanine and my classmates in *Jeanine's Poetry School,* Kathy Pon, Seth Rosenbloom, and Paula Stenberg (Louhi Pohjola) for their comments and suggestions for revisions. I could not have written this book without them.

In addition, the feedback and continued support from the members of my two poetry groups have been critical; my thanks to Judy Aks, Todd Campbell, Bill Hollands, Patricia Joslin, Kim Kralowec, Brooke Lehmann, Caitlin Palo, and Kate Stannard.

Contents

III.

It's not about getting it right.
It's about being open to whatever might arise.

—Pema Chödrön, *True Happiness*

I.

Old Enough

When I was old enough
to carry a jerry can
half full of water

I was sent to the creek
a quarter mile away
to kneel among the pebbles

and feel glacial water
rush past my hands
into the can.

Water sang to metal—
high notes at first, then
deeper, heavier ones.

This is how I remember
it now. Then, I didn't hear
the song of water rushing.

Then, it was not music.
Then, it was the slow trek
back to our A-frame in the woods

the one where hands
were felt in places they
shouldn't have been felt

the place I revise now
to remember only
that the water was cold

and when I knelt
my body knew
song, knew itself.

Reclamation

Come on in
        young self. I see you
peering around the edge of years
                curious yet hesitant.

        How are your scabbed legs
your fingers sticky with pitch
                your body stained
                from fleeing a stepfather's hands?

I recognize your face
        but I've erased much
                of what happened then.

I remember you yearned
        to run and run until you shed the skin
                that covered wounds

but I also remember the caress of aspen leaves, know
        how the cold, clear glacier water in the creek
                released your pain

and I still savor the tang of wild blueberries
        the warm smell of pines. These trail behind us in sparks
                like bioluminescence behind my kayak at night.

I once thought I would banish you
        deny the dark you carried in your gut.
But you would not be silenced, demanded our story
        be told, then retold, to unravel our shawl of shame.

Let me embrace you. Let me assure you that now we are
unbound as we incorporate the past, purge ourselves of blame.

Handed Off

Two hundred years ago in Independence, Missouri,
my great grandmother—too young to know her own drive
toward New, Better, Other—was handed into a covered wagon
and tucked next to hope and hardtack, bacon and the Bible.

At fourteen, she was handed off again, this time to a man
three times her age. But iron spiked her blood and she ran away
to anything other. This I divined from a sepia photo where
she posed with bucket and axe. No man to be seen—

though there must have been one—for I was loved by her daughter,
my grandmother, who cycled through husbands until she met
the man not extinguished by her flame. Grandma handed down
this dis-ease to my mother, who, after my father died,

married a charismatic foreigner. Then it was my turn:
I was handed into their—and my—new life one spring morning
when they traded Montana routine for Alaska adventure.
My first taste of legacy was bitter as bile

but I grew used to the sharp tang. Even now, when I can no longer
ignore my body as I used to, I savor whispers of change.
And my daughter? The night she pried my fingers from
her car door and sped off with her dealer, was she seeking

New, Better, Other? When I handed her off to the latest rehab,
I tucked a love note into her pocket, promised a different life—
for her and for me. How natural it is to default
to what is imprinted on the mind, spine, skin.

The labyrinths of my fingerprints swirl with independence,
resilience, discontent. The age spots on my hands
are signatures of the women before me.
We become more defined every year.

Little Cabin in the Woods

Once there was a cabin built from white spruce
peeled with a drawknife held in the calloused hands
of an Italian immigrant who knew nothing
about building anything. I, his new wife's child,
collected the bent nails he threw to the ground,
pulled fibers from his discarded cigarette butts,
ground his smell into the dirt with my thumbs.

The cabin went up log by log over long Alaskan
summer days. By fall, heat came from a barrel stove,
water from a creek. I thumbed through picture books
by yellow lantern light. On nights when the cold moon
made patterns on the puncheon floor and the howl of wolves
made me tremble, my mother would slip into my bed.
I'd fall asleep with her warm breath upon my hair.

There had been a past. Sunday school, grandparents' laps,
A&W root beer in icy mugs on a car hop tray, my hand
under my grandfather's on his truck's gear stick.
But now was sometime other. Splinters and scabs,
pine pitch, ghostly Northern Lights, and wild sled dogs.
I learned not to miss before, not ask when we were going back,
not cry about the rabbits caught in my stepfather's snares.

Summer rabbits, brown as my teddy bear, were skinned
and cleaned, but the frozen white ones—a thin red line
where the snare wire cut through fur—were hung
over the stove to thaw. At night, they dangled,
spinning slowly in the dark. Once, I saw my stepfather
slit the fur and yank it down over the rabbit's legs.
The fur stuck at the paws, the way my voice stuck
in my throat. Years later, I find an old photograph.
My face is turned upwards.

Wreckage

A moon with *a golden ring* always returns me
to my fourth-grade, linoleum-floored, overheated

Alaskan classroom with its scarred wooden desks,
coat racks stuffed with parkas and boots, and windows

through which I often flew out and over coppery paper birch
and aspen trees to mountaintops and lands where I was not me.

I don't recall the teacher's name, or which rental
the school was near, or even how long before we moved again.

I can, though, still recite parts of the Longfellow poem I chose
to memorize for class, its *wintry sea* and a skipper

who *blew a whiff from his pipe.* Was I drawn to the captain
whose ego lets him think that binding his daughter

to the mast would save her even as he refuses to turn back?
My stepfather convinced me that binding me in lies

as his body erased my childhood would be enough.
How I shivered with recognition when the bound

and freezing daughter exclaims, *O, father!* as she tries
to convince him that what she hears and sees is real.

The best stories are when the flawed get written off the page:
a frozen corpse was he. His hubris—a word I would learn

much later and recognize—his blind and awful
hubris, led to his timely death. I failed at the recital.

I hadn't memorized any lines after the captain dies.
His frozen corpse let me pretend a different ending

where the *little daughter* doesn't drown in the darkness
of her father's sea, where *salt tears* flowed because

she found a way to unknot knots, unfold her wings,
and soar to a place where she could assert: I am.

Paper Fortune Teller

At eleven, my angles soften
and he whose touch I cannot evade
teaches me his truth: rapacious birds
and bees will press against me if
I so much as glance their way.
His hands lurk at the edges
of my days, leave bruises
on and under skin. I learn
to walk head down, numb
to the eyes, the hips of boys.

I begin to believe their scents
would be as his: the damp collar
of an unwashed sweater, pine pitch,
chainsaw oil, sour red wine.
Suffocated, my body deflates—
pierced by ownership.

So, I fold myself into an origami box
like the paper fortune tellers
made by other sixth grade girls
and watch as fingers and thumbs
push me open, close me up,
make me disappear.

First Rise

Sixty-two years after I was lifted into a truck
that would take me and my mother to a place so far north

it might as well have been the moon, I return to the maple-lined
street where my grandparents' house once stood.

Their one-story white 1930s clapboard house (breakfast nook,
green milkshake machine, weeping willow shaded porch)

exists forever in my mind, but now only the light
of the morning sun remains. What did I really expect to find?

My mother had turned toward a fairy tale: adventure, new husband,
anything not Montana. The start of that long ago trip to Alaska

is frozen in a photograph: my grandmother reaches,
as if imploring, into the truck. Her hand on mine is blurred.

The salty taste of missing fills a mouth, distorts time like a canyon
distorts sound. Today, I can smell my grandmother's bread baking,

feel her flour-dusted apron against my cheek. I know now
bread rises before it is punched down.

Undone

My corset yellowed, became frayed with age.
I fashioned it in fury: grommets for laces,
pockets for boning, cords to restrain my rage.

Each cotton panel that bound my bones a page
etched with stories I told myself—even lies
embraced, all the narratives fermented, aged.

From inside my claustrophobic cell, I gauged
every scowl, each word of praise—fickle bases
for marks I scrimshawed on my bones in rage.

Vertebrae under pressure disengage
from those around them. I needed to brace
myself, throw off my corset rotted with age.

I loosed the stays and, one by one, untied aged
cords, felt the sinews of my rage unbraid,
inhaled possibilities freed, uncaged.

Resolution has rusted grommets, set the stage
for rigidness to fail, for openness, grace.
Curiosity now can write a new page.
My skin grows supple without the burn of rage.

Miss Olson at 59

after "Miss Olson," 1952, Andrew Wyeth

Did you ever ask: am I happy?
Your world, this time, is not an open field
but a closed room aged with grime.
Mildew seeps through torn wallpaper
and mixes with stains of wood smoke,
oil lamps, decay. There is no comfort
in the frayed and empty clothesline
above your head, nothing to hang
happiness on. Nothing for me
to envy, and yet, you sit luminous
in a beam of light that caresses
your craggy nose, full lips, the strands
of your hair streaked with gray.
With one gnarled hand, you cradle
a small kitten asleep upon your breast.
You breathe softly, chest rising and falling,
falling and rising. Your gaze is soft, reverent.
Now, I have my answer.

What Do You Remember

my mother asks
of our homesteading days?
We are untangling
necklaces, discarding
shapeless sweaters
and heeled shoes

turning the yellowed pages
of albums filled with snapshots
that play knick-knack on my spine.
Memories careen like marbles
flicked from my fist.

Suddenly, I am six again
learning to map
the steps from our log cabin
to the wooden seat of the outhouse

learning to gauge if my stepfather thinks
it is sunny or if the sky is dark
to judge if his smile is real or a sneer
to dodge his slaps
to not say
I miss my grandparents' house
a million miles away.

I learn. I learn to accompany him tearless
to check for rabbits in his snares
to remain tearless
when Northern Lights unsettle night
and drench my walls
with eerie pulsing light.

All these appear in dreams even now.
I can't throw them away
can't cart them off to Goodwill.

I probably remember things
in ways you don't, I tell her.
What would be the point
of admitting I yearned
for a sky beyond my sky

that I still wish to un-remember
I was erased
amid the sparse trees
and unrelenting snow.

She was the bride of adventure
a prospector for the promise
of a different life.

I just happened to be there.
I was only six,
I say.

It's hard to know
what I remember.

On the Brink

I played hopscotch with shadows cast by an old cabin decaying
in the forest. Light, dark. Sun quaked through aspen leaves.

My mother still read me fairy tales; I resisted the cabin's dark door.
Then, one afternoon, I was drawn towards the cobwebbed opening

and crossed the threshold. Light leaked through grimed windows.
Yellowed scraps of paper mildewed on the wooden floor. Tin cans,

labels gone, spilled from a shelf. Askew on a metal bed frame,
a stained blue and white striped mattress wept cotton.

The iron stove door hung open, and maps sagged on the walls.
No curtains. I recognized despair—its ghost hung in the air.

I backed away from the smell of rot, the dead of dust on my skin,
retreated until I could feel ground, solid, under my feet again—

then ran until I was rescued by the sun. It was the last time I played
hopscotch. How quickly one's world becomes undone.

Alaska Revelation 9.2

I'd been well prepared. I knew the stories
of Moses smiting the Red Sea, a sandaled Jesus

reviving the dead, angels that appeared silent
as white tigers. I made nightly pleas for soul-keeping

(*if I should die before I wake*) and I listened
to my mother hum *How Great Thou Art* while she tested

the steam iron with her tongue-moistened finger.
So I was ready that Good Friday in 1964

when *awesome wonder* arrived. No warning,
then a roar like Gabriel rehearsing for the big day:

wood walls screamed, doors shrieked
glass splintered, plates slid, shattered.

Even our Bible thudded to the floor.
And the earth roared and heaved and shook.

I heard the *rolling thunder,* staggered
across the bottomless floor, clasped my hands

and fell to my knees where I promise-prayed
like a revival tent convert. Through shivering

windows, I saw birds soar into the distant heavens
that gazed, unmoved, upon my kneeling form

and I learned then what was truly meant by
power throughout the universe displayed.

Hunger

Beyond the upper branches of the rusty-leafed willows,
I imagine the sky is that impossible blue of skies

in Little Golden Books: the kind of blue under which other kids
ride bikes past numbered mailboxes that anchor paved driveways.

No paved driveways or bicycles here under my blue.

There's a marshy area next to our rental with heaps of dead leaves,
old tires, broken brown bottles, mildewed cardboard boxes.

On the other side of this marsh, lives a girl my age. Her last name
does not end with a vowel. Her parents do not slam doors or fists.

And this perfection of a girl has a turquoise Easy-Bake Oven
complete with tiny packages of cake mix and miniature pans.

When she lets me hold them, I can feel what it's like to ride
down paved streets where people wave, call you by your name.

One day, I crawl through the girl's unlocked playroom window,
steal her mixes and pans, and make a batter so rich and sweet

I can taste that other blue, feel pavement, smooth under my wheels.

What I Want

my mother and I collect fall leaves
scatter them across her glass table
skeletal ribs and yellow edges
veins glow in afternoon sun   and then

What do you want?   she gestures at
carvings of walruses and seals
a blue Meissen bowl   pewter plates
a pottery vase I gave her sixty years ago

Your mahogany chest
        but what I mean is I want me age three leaning against
        that ornate chest my mother's majorette's baton raised
        in one hand & my feet splendid in white cowboy boots

I don't remember this   it's a warmth forged
from a framed black and white displayed
on her bookcase   a snapshot taken before I learned

batons bruise   boots kick hate   before I learned
wooden boxes hold more than faded corsages
old baby blankets   certificates of birth

before I notice that my mother's hands
resemble veined and fragile leaves

In Praise of Glacial Movement

for my mother

You deform with careful, deliberate
slowness—creaking, groaning—the weight of years
pressing, making you firm and obdurate,
strong in your convictions but dammed by fear
that leaves you jumbled in the meltwater
of conversation. Your surface, once smooth
is blemished now with blue shadows, furrowed
and dotted with the memories of youth,
the accumulated debris of life
lived long and well. But on those clear mornings
when your equilibrium line is high
and the light shimmers off the crystalline
caves of your mind, you sparkle, flow, and glide—
surging still, suffused with life magnified.

Minor Key

My mother has always
loved music
needs it
like her snow-
covered mountains
need
the calcite light
of the moon
to sparkle
on cold Alaskan nights

a melody begins
her eyes undull
and she sways
to the pulse
of flamenco guitars
a violin's soft cry

winter's unending dark
fades to reveal
a Spanish plaza
where men gaze
into women's eyes
and hands caress hips

so when her world
judders and stops
and she asks
if she can
take her CDs
to the home

I hear
the dead quiet
of a room
empty
of minor keys
and I say
    I'll pack your songs
    I'll send you enough
    to wrap you in sunlight

Named by All

I've stood still—bereft—unable to remember
my name even when I search for it in the shrill
cry of an osprey, a stream rippling its banks,
the whisper of pine boughs. Too often,
all I hear is the muffled monotone of loss

droning between sky and rock, between my spine
and sternum, like the buzz a dying fly makes
as its legs claw air. In these moments,
when I am lost in an alien world with others
who yearn to reclaim their children from the realm

of hungry ghosts, I must unmask
and walk curious into here and now, attend only
to breath, lean into possibilities nascent
in the tight, pink buds on a rhododendron bush,
in the eggs of a song sparrow, and accept, no,

not merely accept, but comprehend, that I am not
trapped between is and isn't. Ospreys and flies,
the ache for a lost child, the recurrence
of growth, bright and green, on the tips of boughs
in spring—I am named by all I encounter.

II.

Elemental

after Carl Phillips

To hear above the frothing river's symphony the full-throat roar
of a Kodiak brown bear who realizes a male is threatening
her two small cubs, to see her turn, salmon blood streaming
from her muzzle as she rears up, charges, curved claws swiping
his flank, his shoulder, to witness how she throws her furred
head back and summons a sound so elemental you feel it
at the base of your skull—a sound you recognize because
you made it once when your daughter wrenched her soft hand
from yours and slid into her dealer's car—to cover your eyes
when, despite wounds given and received, one cub is lost,
this is when you remember—in your flesh and sinew, in the
surge of your pulse—how it feels to be a mother who howls.

November Storm, Cloud Mountain Retreat

who knew
rain could hold
so much
weight

as it batters the roof
of the room
where I sit
pummeled

by echoes
of water splashing
under a child's
yellow rubber boots

Bardo

Earth
You were born,
made flesh of my flesh,
made body with birth
onto this world
you chose to reject
as you hurled yourself
toward the void
year after year.

Water
At twelve you began
to bleed with a need
I could not understand.
You sought others
to feed the hungry ghost
coiled inside your belly.
Salt leached from my eyes
and my thirst for you
grew parallel to yours.

Fire
When I found foil
blackened with residue,
my heart was singed.
The dragon sang
its siren song to you
and you succumbed:
eyes half shut,
your cheeks burning.

Air
You evaporated time,
intangible as the emptiness
of dead space left after
you hurled curses at me,
after a slammed front door,
after telephone calls
false with promises.
I forgot how to breathe.

Void
This gap, this
black space, it lies
between us
and has grown
to such an abyss
that were we to step
towards each other I fear
we would fall forever.
Would that this void
held a veil we could tear
from time so we could
pass into another world
free from craving
for the other.

Dear Hungry Ghost

The day you hitched a ride out
of my life and into an alien world

my knees shattered the floorboards.
I had been taught to pray past despair

as if prayer was currency, and solace
could be bought with a wallet

filled with supplications. I offered pleas
and bargains, stacked them until they reached

from foundation to the roof, and still
I could not buy you back. Spent, I bowed

to the incalculable, took one deep breath
for me, then one for you.

No exchange of anything: breath releasing
me and you, my beloved hungry ghost.

Summer Afternoon

blossoms on the red buckeye tree
droop detach fall they do this
every year and yet every year
        I am surprised by dying

already my hands miss the way
I've cupped upturned faces
of petals marveled how
        the bright red panicles

jutting from tall stems thrust their ruby
throats through foliage thirst
for the tongue of a bee to whisper
        honeyed promises

of splendor eternal but what if
everything clung stubborn forever
unchanged can we really cherish
        what cannot die

Lamentation Ghazal

Addiction darkens the early hours of the morning
bringing me to solitary grief, invisible in my mourning.

Curse the scourge of heroin and methamphetamine,
demons that diminish my daughter, deny me this morning.

Even the rising sun whose rays caress the windowpane
fails before it reaches me. For her, I am in mourning.

God toys with us, dangles "daughter" on a chain,
holds her between life and death in my mind this morning.

I wear blame like prison garb, continue to maintain
jurors would find me guilty. I sentence myself to mourning.

Keening, I repent of errors made that stain
love and leave me yearning for her each morning.

Mothers like me tally their transgressions, paint
numerous vignettes of opportunities lost, insist on mourning.

Over years, hope erodes like a mountain washed with rain.
Prayer becomes stuck as if frozen by a winter morning.

Queries (how are you? where are you?) again and again
result in lies and more lies. They spiral me deeper into mourning.

Sometimes she surfaces suddenly like a fast-moving hurricane,
tempestuous and turbulent, as if to regain every lost morning.

Until she disappears, her energy spent, her intent drained,
veins crying in complaint—for their dark nourishment, mourning.

When, finally, from bed I rise, I inhale all the possibility of pain,
exhale the possibilities of life, breathe so I can meet the morning.

You might say I'm blind to hope (addicted to shame), that I'm a
zealot whose name begins with sin. However, this is my mourning.

How to Pronounce *Grief*

Go ahead. Say it slow
so that it begins
in the throat. You need
to close the muscles
around the sound
as if to trap it there
for as long as you can
before your tongue touches
the softness of your palate,
your voice escapes,
and *grief* begins:
hard *g*, howl of *r*,
then the *eeee* that travels
into your mouth to lodge
between your teeth
and pull your cheeks
in a travesty of a smile.
Your breath flows out,
sends the final *fffff*
across your lips and off
into a space you are still
trying to understand.

January in the Park

finally, a day
drenched with light
so bright

you must raise
a hand to shield
yourself and still

you hear
the bare-branched aspen
scrape against endless blue

as if to ask
does heaven exist
after all the snow

that bent and broke
even the sturdy
rock roses

as if to ask
can you believe
in after-snow

when all you hear
is scratching

Second Rise

I do not want to rise this morning, pull on my robe whose pockets
are crammed with notes on how to steady the trembling of hands.

I know bread requires a first rise and then a punching down
to deflate the dough so it can proof, become resilient. But deflation

takes breath away: the 2 a.m. phone call from my son—
his girlfriend left him, he needs to get away, can I take his cat?

And there's the doctor's appointment I've put off, and headlines
that decry the destruction of what I thought indestructible.

My son's Maine Coon cat, hungry and impatient, is not interested
in any of this. His giant paws knead my chest, prepping my body

for a second proofing. He is telling me he needs me, and this
becomes my sustenance. That we act in response to others matters.

Water for a drooping red geranium, a smile for a barista, a call
to say *I love you,* opening a can of chicken and rice for the cat.

Still Life with Bulldozers and Backhoes

In the empty lot
across the street
they graze on ground
scrape and grind—
diesel sculptors
of land and sound
that rumble words
shatter lines I try to write
take up residence
between my shoulder blades and teeth.

Then it's quitting time
and quiet unfurls through air.
Into this gap
this negativity of sound—
an echo, insistent:
how the backhoe's motor
idled, revved, and whined,
how metal screamed
when it hit rock,
how workers' voices floated
like dandelion seeds
windblown

this stillness opens

silence

then

words
asking to be heard

The Lighthouse

I climb toward
El Faro Viejo
whose bold red
and white bands once
warned sailors away.
At night the flashing light
winks like a crystal ball
with only two answers.

I pass stately cardóns
centuries old,
torotes with papery
bark that shivers
in the breeze,
and coralita vines
whose heart-shaped leaves,
pink flowers, and soft
green tendrils smother
the plants they cling to.

The vines are also known
as chains of love.
I've forged those chains:
clutched too hard
(pleaded, *but I love*)—
then changed the locks
when love escaped from me.

I no longer know
who is free and I am left
like a coralita-bound cardón
with brittle limbs
that fracture in the wind.

Up close
the red bands
of the lighthouse flake.
The white paint
is dirty, yellowed.
Is everything scarred
by what touches it?
What doesn't have
scratches, dents,
and fractures under
surfaces of
flowers, skin,
steel, and stone?

I suspect
the lighthouse winks
not with answers,
but at the joke
that anything loved
can remain
undamaged.

Running in the Dark

Religion is asking the question, "What if?"
—Nick Cave, *Faith, Hope and Carnage*

flashlight forgotten
        body follows path but can't
                avoid unseen puddles

diagonal rain
        flashes white static between
                streetlights   empty sidewalks

winter branches scrape
        hieroglyphic messages
                against flat pre-dawn sky

trail ahead is faint
        without stars dark shadows loom
                damp decay fouls the air

breath and pulse mirror
        rhythm of hymns and prayers
                flung heavenward—a plea:

what if   what if   what if
        what if that question is both
                call and response

Between the Lines

after David Wagoner

I've stood still—
yes, lost at times—
amid the anonymity of trees,
hoping to be found
by the shrill cry
of a peregrine falcon,
a stream rippling its bank,
the warm fragrance of pine boughs.

Too often, all I hear
is the muffled monotone
of my own thoughts
meandering between parallel lines.
Nothing appears
and I am truly lost—
until I trail my hands
through tall grass, feel

the blessing of dew
upon my fingers,
and affirm nothing is lost here,
here where there's a chance
to meet a powerful stranger
who offers
a fountain pen,
the nib filled with ink.

A Walk in the Park

The twins are not looking ahead.
Their small right hands reach
out from the tandem stroller
to stroke wheat-blonde winter stalks
of tall beach grass. Their parents
are focused on discerning
the safe, the prudent path
on the uneven sidewalk.
The toddlers' fingers brush drops
of rain that cling to the reeds.
They bring their hands to their mouths,
spread sky kisses on their lips,
taste earth's sweetness on their tongues.

Seal of Delight

I'm doing my slow
old-lady jog
to keep
synapses firing
and prevent
sneaker waves
of age from sucking
me under, when
I hear a splash
and see a harbor seal
shoot out of Elliott Bay,
a vertical, smooth
black cylinder of joy—
okay, maybe it is just
a seal trying to catch a fish
but it looks like joy to me—
and I decide
I'll go with that,
this will do:
the seal surfaces,
leaps, huffs,
a wet splash
of body, tail, flippers,
then one last
thrust of muscle
up and up, and I swear
the seal laughs
while yellow kelp
trails from her mouth

and a million tiny
droplets of sea water
cascade like silver sparks
from a risen god.

Faith and Science

You could say it was a coincidence.
A few days after I placed my hand on the warm
smooth branch of a Baja torote tree,
closed my eyes and sent my pulse down
its trunk and roots, underground
from desert seedling to desert seedling,
then across the enzymatic fingers of furred fungi
to wild blue lupine beside mountain lakes,
to shivering sugar pines in dense forests,
to where I imagine my daughter lives,
my heart-waves surging so that she might feel
a sudden warmth enfold her,
she called to tell me nothing and everything
I needed, at that moment, to hear.

Here in the Land Where Desert Meets the Sea

where magenta bougainvillea cascades over
adobe walls and yellow orioles chatter
above my hammock, the morning should be
suffused with promise, yet I wear discontent
that itches like a wool sweater on a winter day.

I am born of women dissatisfied: Great-grandmother
ran toward the place where she could wield her own axe,
and Grandma tried on husbands until she found
one her size. My mother moved from house to house,
sought reinvention when new became old.

My daughter felt this disquiet. She was so restless
she strode right off the stage to dance with needles
and dealers whose very currency was change.

And I, who try so hard to breathe in *here and now,*
am pulled by strings of DNA across miles and years,
threads that curl and bind like the creeping vines
that strangle cacti and desert trees.

Can I rid myself of ghosts who whisper and suggest?
Can my daughter break the ties before
she is overwhelmed?

Here where desert meets sea, I reach for
a kind of alchemy: a small moment to rest,
appreciate now a tiny crab peering from a hole,
now, a giant frigatebird soaring on thermals, and now,
to know this brief interlude as enough.

III.

A Wake

after "Wake" by Richard Serra, Olympic Sculpture Park

Beside,
behind, in front—
water transmuted
into steel—not waves
but the wake
from something unseen,
this fusion of iron and carbon
and the very air we breathe,
all tempered by fire, then cast
upon our gravel beach,
sinuous curves
culminating in
knife edges.

I cannot find
the way forward.
In this canyon, this abyss,
heaven above offers no light.
I careen off walls, barriers that multiply
every time I consider the latest
lies, distortions, egregious
actions by those
who purport
to lead.

Vessels
of hatred create
wakes that foul
beaches and bodies,
leave oil slicks that coat
the mind, clog the brain,
make fists want to
smash.

How do I
resist this force
that blinds, deafens
makes me dumb? How do I
navigate steel walls rusted by
generations of tears, rage? I look
for light and find it—not above—
but in the gaps, in narrow fissures
through which the sun's rays
seep, reach down to caress
the ground, summon
new life.

If I stand
quite still, eschew
the hollowness of falsehoods,
allow my body to sense the undulations
in the path, I can start to discern a way forward
despite what churns the unseen sea.
A wake, after all,
is a consequence.
I can choose
my response.

Crow Shrouded in Geraniums

At the edge of the sidewalk
under a gray-barked ash tree
lies the still intact carcass
of a small common black crow.

I would have missed it, thought it
just another discarded
black plastic bag, soiled t-shirt,
broken-soled shoe, if not for
pink geranium petals
someone had scattered over
the dark remains—tenderly

the way a mother blows palm
kisses to a departing
child. The blossoms rest upon
the breast as if to welcome
the crow from sky to dust. Damp
with recent rain, they transform

the dusky crow into an
explosion of color once
foreign to its nature, but
now its essence, florescence.

I see the petals were plucked
from a nearby bush growing
by a fence. Above, silent
mourners perch on a black bough.

Imagine My Surprise

when my stepfather, dead
and duly buried, reappeared

as a large black spider
splayed upon the wall

above my bed. He crouched there
unmoving, as if waiting for the chance

to fall and tangle his long legs
in the folds of my new sheets,

leave tiny barbed black hairs
upon the pillow like shavings

of the beard he wore.
I watch and twitch

with the need to run away, or
squash the monstrosity and observe

his liquids mix with shattered parts that leave
a stain upon the wall, my sheets, my eyes.

Moonrise, Baja California Sur

Between the cupped palms of the hills beyond the arroyo,
the moon ascends, casts her pearled light across sand, cardóns,
torotes, and ocotillos, across the late minutes of the afternoon
until it reaches the final rays of the descending sun.

To stand in the in-between is to stand in awe of the unknown.
I spread my arms, one toward the moon, the other reaching
for the sun. Mind pull of one; blood heat of the other. Briefly,
I am the moon, sun, sky, and the land upon which I stand.

Besos del Cielo

They're rare—these revelations—they come
at you sideways, slam you in the solar plexus
when they appear. You could be sitting on a bus
working on your Spanish by eavesdropping
as three chatty women balance packages
on their laps and share plans for Navidad.

This leads you to think about Christmas and God
and how you take pride in that you are *spiritual*—
you certainly do not believe in some old patriarch
who randomly dispenses blessings and afflictions.

You believe, instead—well, you aren't entirely sure,
but it feels good, what you think you believe in.
You remember you cried at 1 a.m. on Haleakalā
to see stars above *and* below you, that Vavilov's
Ave Maria makes you tremble as you sense
a shimmering mystery just beyond.

The women move to the exit, and you notice
a forgotten purse. Before you can say anything,
a young man in a hoodie snatches the purse and runs
for the door. He hands the purse to the women,
returns to his seat. People murmur, shift, look
at one another, nod to the young man.

And there it is again, in your knees,
in the palms of your hands, on your tongue
that remembers, *hallowed be thy name*,
and you know you need more of it.

Perfume Bottle on the Windowsill

The last thing left in my great aunt's room
is a half-empty bottle of Chanel No. 5
silhouetted against the suffocating gloom

of gray light seeping into the bedroom.
Relentless raindrops falling from eaves deprive
us of grace. The only sound in that old room

is this incessant beat, like drums before a tomb.
At the road's far edge, a grove of Southern live
oaks stand silhouetted against the sky's dark gloom.

An overgrown lawn threatens to consume
several Adirondack chairs that have survived,
aged, like those of us in our great aunt's room.

Those chairs seated generations from bridegrooms
to newborns and mourners. Now, Chanel revives
memories that arrive as antidotes against gloom.

The salty scent of sorrow mingles with perfume,
chairs, and rain to remind us that we strive
to keep alive what we hold dear. In Great Aunt's room
we pass like shadows through gray cashmere gloom.

The Art of Projection

What do whales dream of
as they float in half-brain sleep

one hemisphere a blank slate
while the other remains alert

like a nervous parent listening
for breath, non-breath?

Do they imagine
smooth-skinned, salt-flecked cows

with long, slender pectoral fins,
fecund, flirtatious?

Perhaps they dream of muscular bulls,
flukes broad and scarred,

their songs reverberating
like Gregorian chants through water?

Or maybe their fantasies
are of calves who can

breathe on their own,
who will launch themselves

into air while droplets of water
flash silver in the sun?

On board the speeding Zodiac
with our *Cabo Adventure* guide

who shouts out whale info bits
like a Maritime Bingo caller,

we clamor for just one more breach,
just one more thunderous fin slap,

just one more heart stopping swoosh
as breath fountains into the sky—

one more chance to project
ourselves onto another

Eagle Atop the P.I. Globe in Seattle

I usually don't even notice the trade sign for the defunct
newspaper. It sits on the roof of an office building
across the railroad tracks from a city park I visit daily.

But on this first day of January, I am searching for an omen
of what the new year will bring. So, when I spot a live,
white-plumed eagle perched on its metal double

atop the steel and neon globe, I stop to take a photo,
proof I've witnessed an augury, a clear message
that it will be a majestic year—a double eagle year—

provided I am sharp-eyed and don't let myself get too ruffled.
Just then, a single shrieking crow dive bombs the eagle.
She is joined by another, then another, until

the attacks from the murder of crows become vicious.
The beleaguered bird leaves his perch and hides
his great body in a densely branched tree.

Not even his head is visible. It's only the first day of 2025.
I think I'll keep searching for another sign. The trick
is recognizing it when I see it, and I can be selective.

Baja Layers

You kneel, thrust your fingers into the sand
of the land you visit de vez en cuando
and reach beneath the glittery, gated resorts
whose glass reflects the waves of dólares
that crash upon the playas, beneath
the rich-green golf courses where sprinklers
cast rainbows against the sky, beneath
umbrellaed beach clubs adorned with cacti
and torote trees transplanted from the desert

and, deeper, touch the granite bedrock
that was here when the Baja split from México,
when the Pericú dove for pearls, when Jesuits gifted
pestilence, when piratas hid in coves to plunder
Spanish galleons—a world once filled
with rattlesnakes, coyotes, scorpions,
golden eagles, cougars, and great horned owls.
Now, bulldozers clear the way for concrete block,
crushing granite and the burrows of desert pocket mice.

We can be blinded by yearning for what was.
So much beneath, sí, and yet so much above, here.
You brush sand from your hands, resume your walk.
The branch of a torote scrapes your arm—
you hear it hum, thin, airy, like the wail of an ocarina.

Mira, m'ija, it seems to say: how fragile my papery bark.
See how it peels, curls, is blown across the desert
like centuries across this Baja sand. But see, too,
how solid my trunk, how strong my roots.
The shadow of my twining limbs will dance
no matter how ancient, how modern la luz.

Same Old Sunrise

Today's was just like yesterday's—and all the days before that—
and I expect it will be the same tomorrow. See how the sun

paints—again—with the thinnest of brushes, a band of light
in that valley between the far peaks, then, shy

as a kindergartner on the first day of school, slides behind
a mountaintop before it emerges, beaming, bounding

with energy. And it's not just the sunrise. This morning, palm trees
are still weaving their fingers through languid tropical air

and fallen bougainvillea bracts continue to tumble across the desert
floor, colors bursting, in a botanical game of chase. And look

at that mourning dove perched on the branch of her favorite cactus.
She calls and calls as if to awaken the dead.

Even the creamy white trumpet of the desert thornapple blares
sameness with its white bell that calls insects to prayer. Dewdrops

cling to its sides like fire opal studs in a young girl's ear. Desire
to skim pages can blind the reader. Constancy is a curse

only for those who seek next, next. There's a slight brown curling
at the edge of the thornapple, and look, look,

there's a spider spinning a web between flower and leaf.

A Necessary Ekphrasis

The upper edge of the frame is Cabo azul wisped with white.
Pebbled sand and speckled granite anchor the bottom,
a wind-frothed Pacific is on the left, and, on the right,
a banked arroyo curves, scooped out by summer rains
that rush from the Sierra de la Lagunas. What is framed
is worthy of the Met, even the marbled walls of St. Peter's.
See how everything reaches towards the sky to receive blessings?
Light falls on the aloe vera's plump golden tubes where bees gorge
on pollen, the leaves of the spiked blue agave gather dew,
and a desert wren is portrayed on the top branch of a flame tree
bedecked with slender, elongated green seed pods. Two ancient
gnarled cactuses appear like sentinels around the center symbol:
a bougainvillea bush so bright it might burst into flame.
We are who we are, it seems to announce. *Out of dust*
we all reach for a brief moment of heaven.

Sitting Zazen

I lower myself to the cushion,
feel my hips, my back resist

as I struggle to cede dominion.
I consider my mind, see it twist

and twirl like a ribbon in the wind—
each dip a regret, every rise

a decision I'd like to amend.
Distractions beckon, so do lies.

I embrace them all as they appear—
thoughts are mere fables constructed of air.

I breathe in the heavy poison of grief,
then exhale and concede this belief:

the mind is supple as leaves of spring grass,
each blade a story to simply let pass.

Seat of Belonging

Even though the roots of my hair are gray,
like my mother and aunts once did, I rise
early every morning to greet the first rays
of light, light the day's fires, stir syllables
and words for my children so that I might
nourish them the way I used to do in those
early hours when we were folded together
in a wooden rocking chair, wrapped in the
orange, umber, and ruby red herringbone
blanket crocheted by my mother's mother
while she waited, sleepless, for my birth.

Wooden rocking chair
cradles two bodies swaddled.
Blaze of fall colors.

Bonanza, 1959

My grandparents' house had the kind of safety
you feel when you don't have to think about safety,
solid and deep as my grandfather's brown recliner.
The house smelled of fried chicken and oatmeal cookies,
and the tall aluminum coffee pot never ran out of welcome.

When my mom would drop me off on Saturday nights,
it was *Bonanza* time: ice cream in milky-green glass bowls
atop TV tray tables, the holey feel of the doilies
guarding my grandfather's chair, his gnarled hands
that smelled of sawdust and machine oil from his shop.

Ben Cartwright, Adam, Hoss, and Little Joe
appeared, and we would lean forward with the gallop
of *Bonanza*'s theme song, lean into the vast skies
of a ranch that would survive every challenge—
predictable as the scoops of Rocky Road in my dish.

I was sure it would always be, didn't know then
that a finger with a new ring could change the channel.
Years afterward, I'd replay these episodes, refuse revision.
Some things cannot be amended by stories traded later
around holiday tables. They are kept in pockets,

caressed like talismans. I remember I'd feign sleep
on the couch until my mother returned. I remember
the faint scents of cedar and dust and aging wood.
I remember I rubbed the satin border of the evening
between my fingers.

Last Rise

Each small bear begins the same: flour for substance, yeast for
breath, sugar for character, and milk. All young bears need milk.

There's also a teaspoon of salt for common sense, eggs to remind
that what's inside counts, and, most important, cardamom—

a spice that calms the mind, invites clarity, increases joy, and acts
as a protective charm, or so I've read recently. When my two kids

still appeared on Christmas mornings in footed pjs, I didn't know
as much. Now I recognize the aroma of intangible hope.

Those early years, the crumb was moist and soft and we all wanted
just one more minute smeared with butter, dipped in honey.

These later years, there are fewer of us around the table;
the yeast seems less potent, the bread, often heavy, is not improved

by jam, sprinkles of sugar. Nevertheless, I still get up early
every Christmas morning to mix and knead, let the dough rise

in a well-oiled bowl, then knead it again before shaping the small
bears—yes, even now when only one child can come.

I haven't cut the recipe in half. This morning, as I proof the bears,
I remember this last rise is crucial—it takes vigilance to prevent

an irreversible fall. The alchemy of kneading and proofing is
known to all who yearn to shape and offer sustenance.

Hunger changes, but, every year, I offer the promise
of cardamom Christmas bears. This is what love tastes like.

Shedding Weight

All this splendid green
and the promise of a true blue
sky keep you moving forward

and yet you carry a bulky pack
into which you've crammed
every map and script you've used

and every map and script you think
you need to move ahead. Its weight
slows you, deepens the crease between

your eyes. You're sure you must keep
those old pages about your stepfather
in whose hands you were a phantom

until you drew a map for your escape.
And there's the plan you kept revising
for your daughter, the one she burned

when she learned to play with fire.
And the map you completed for your son
who found it flawed and tattooed his own maps

on his torso, hands, and legs.
All those papers led to here, but
what if you threw them all away?

What could your life be without
the weight that keeps you
so grimly focused?

Perhaps you might feel,
for even the briefest moment,
a more bearable lightness.

About the Author

Cindy Buchanan grew up in Alaska, has a B.A. in English from Gonzaga University, and studies poetry with Jeanine Walker. She is a member of two monthly poetry groups and lives in Seattle. Her work has been published in *ONE ART, Hole in the Head Review, The Inflectionist Review, Cirque,* and other journals. Her poetry has been nominated for *Best of the Net*. Her chapbook is *Learning to Breathe* (Finishing Line Press, 2023).

Find her at:
cindybuchanan.com

www.ingramcontent.com/pod-product-compliance
Lightning Source LLC
LaVergne TN
LVHW090534110826
845146LV00003B/1098

* 9 7 9 8 9 0 1 4 6 7 1 4 5 *